Prayers for the Sick

Other books by Michael Hollings and Etta Gullick

The One Who Listens
It's Me, O Lord
The Shade of His Hand
You Must Be Joking Lord
Morning and Night Prayers

by Michael Hollings

Day by Day
I Will Be There
A Catholic Prayer Book
Pastoral Care of Homosexuals

by Etta Gullick

Getting To Know You

Prayers for the Sick

by
MICHAEL HOLLINGS
and
ETTA GULLICK

MAYHEW-McCRIMMON
Great Wakering, Essex

First published in Great Britain in 1976 by
MAYHEW-McCRIMMON LTD
Great Wakering   Essex

©Copyright 1976 by Michael Hollings and
Etta Gullick

ISBN 0-85597-162-2

Reprinted 1978

Cover design: Paul Chilvers

Printed by Mayhew-McCrimmon

INTRODUCTION

As each of us is unique, we cannot fully share an experience of pain with anyone else when suffering even something as common as a cold, or a headache. You have probably had these at one time or another— we have! We could describe them to you vividly, but even if we recalled your pain for you, it would be your pain recalled for you, and ours for us.

Nevertheless, we come close enough to have some sharing, and so some sympathy; though the less experience of a particular pain, the less easy it is to realise what another is going through. How can we, who, up till now, have not suffered arthritus, know the pain of those who can scarcely move from a chair? How can we who are not blind sense the pain of blindness, or the blanket of deafness, or the helplessness of the mentally disturbed?

So when we are trying to share we can often only say 'I know pain' rather than; 'I know your pain'. Therefore, you see, it is important in the brotherhood of man that we all, being born into a world of pain, in some degree experience it too.

Again what extraordinarily differing effects pain has on people! We ponder about the existence of pain, but there is also the perennial problem that some people can 'take it', and others apparently cannot. For it is true that the crucible of suffering purifies and enobles some in such a way that the person, like Job, seems 'to hear the voice of God in the tempest' and positively radiate peace, joy and life; and others seem to shrivel and grow daily more bitter.

The Christian facing pain faces it with Christ. That is easy to say, but less easy to live. This does not mean Stoic endurance; it is pain suffered, pain fought, pain accepted, and in a sense pain defeated. The un-understandable element is not removed, but the figure of the suffering Christ somehow penetrates an inner part of us and leads us to greater endurance in a sense a more living, a more fully human reaction. All the same we are normally left asking either 'Why should *I* suffer?' or 'Why should *they* suffer?'

It is time-wasting for us to discuss this here at a reasoning, intellectual level. Certainly we can pursue ideas, but answers are elusive and unsatisfactory. Only by concentrating on God, experiencing him in Christ in yourself, and continuing to live openly and closely to your own pain or those who suffer does there come some knowledge. It is not easy to put in words, but we hope you will come to know what we are getting at in your own facing of pain.

If you truly love God, the pain does not go away, but you live more fully and in a way which can only be experienced. This new dimension in which that figure on the cross through pain and death grows glorious, joyous, and intensely loving in the resurrection.

Lord, the cross has so many meanings, but for me at this moment it is only by looking at you there and letting my pain be joined with yours that I can keep going. I do not know how this happens, but your sufferings make mine bearable and somehow almost understandable. My helplessness is no longer hopeless for you share the burden with me and your silent love brings love into my sufferings. Lord, remain with me in my distress and help me to comfort others in pain.

Lord Jesus,
You know what pain is like.
You know
    the torture of the scourge upon your back,
    the sting of the thorns upon your brow,
    the agony of the nails in your hands.
You know what I'm going through just now.
Help me
    to bear my pain
    gallantly, cheerfully and patiently,
And help me to remember
    that I will never be tried
    above what I am able to bear,
    and that you are with me,
    even in this valley of the deep dark shadow.
In ev'ry pang that rends the heart,
The Man of Sorrows had a part;
He sympathises with our grief,
And to the suff'rer sends relief.

William Barclay

Praise to you, O Christ, and honour and glory! As your passion drew near, you began to know weariness and depression. So you took upon yourself the weakness of our human nature, that you might strengthen and console those who are fearful of serious illness. I beseech you to free me from all destructive sadness. Grant that all I have so far endured may be to your glory. Deliver me from faint-heartedness and all unreasonable fears, and fix my heart firmly and unwaveringly on you.

Now, my gentle Lord, I know that for me to live out gracefully the example of your passion is a desire close to your heart. Therefore I will for the future try to imitate that example rather than complain as I have done . . . Do you now teach me.

Henry Suso (1295-1399)

Use of pain

We ask thee not, O Lord, to rid us of pain; but grant us in thy mercy that our pain may be free from waste, unfretted by rebellion against thy will, unsoiled by thought of ourselves, purified by love of others and ennobled by devotion to thy kingdom, through the merits of thine only Son, our Lord.

Henry S. Nash

Suffering and the risen Christ

O God, who hast exhalted the Crucified, thy Son, by a triumphant resurrection and ascension into heaven: may his triumphs and glories so shine in the eyes of our hearts and minds, that we may more clearly comprehend his sufferings, and more courageously pass through our own; for his sake who with thee and the Holy Ghost liveth and reigneth, one God, for ever and ever.

Eric Milner-White (1884–1964)

Risen Lord, I thank you for being with me. Help me always to remember that you have triumphed over death and pain, and that in your power and strength, we can over come all our fears. I praise and thank you with my lips; deepen my praise so that it will touch my heart and that through your power the whole of me will be healed. Amen.

For the power to suffer and to triumph

O God,
I don't want anything startling or heroic;
I just want to be able to bear things.
They can do a lot for me,
but sometimes even their drugs don't work.
Help me to bear things
    without grumbling;
    without complaining;
    without whining;
    without self-pity,
    like a good soldier.
Help me
    to pass the breaking point and not break,
You know all about it, Lord Jesus.

9

You knew
the mental agony of Gethsemane.
You knew
the physical pain of the lash,
of the crown of thorns, of the nails.
I know you won't mind me saying
that I am glad you went through it all,
because it means that you can understand
exactly how I feel.
I know that in the end
all things pass;
Till then, make me brave,
I wait for your promise of the time
when there shall be no more pain.
The Psalmist said:
I kept my faith, even when I said, I am greatly
afflicted.
Help me too to keep my faith.

William Barclay

The help of the Holy Spirit in suffering

Vouchsafe, good Lord, that as thou hast sent this sickness unto me, so thou wouldest likewise be pleased to send thy Holy Spirit into my heart, whereby this present sickness may be sanctified unto me, that I may use it as thy school, wherein I may learn to know the greatness of my misery and the riches of thy mercy; that I may be so humbled at the one that I despair not of the other; and that I may so renounce all confidence of help in myself, or in any other creature, that I may only put the whole of my salvation in all thy sufficient merits. Amen.

Lewis Bayley (1565–1631)

Pain

Lord, have mercy! What more can I say with this intolerable pain which grips me? I suppose it was like this on the cross? Your humanity cried out 'Why'—and I, crucified by pain join you, Lord.

I offer it for all mankind and particularly those dear to me whose needs I know. I cannot think or act as I would, but let the bearing of this pain be my prayer. It cannot go on for ever, for either it will get worse and kill me, or there will come relief. Lord, thy will be done. Whatever it may be—Lord, have mercy.

Colin Stephenson

I am overwhelmed by pain, and my failure to bear it well; my heart is cold and my mind distracted. I offer all my suffering and failure to you to be united with your Son's cross and passion. I am nothing and have nothing except the pain; do what you want with it and me.

I hurt again, Lord,
I hurt all over.
From the very onset of my sickness I rebelled against
     pain,
I hid behind my medicine bottles,
I threw myself at you in what must have been pure
     melodrama, begging a reprieve.
Yet somehow you must have seen something valuable

about pain because it is still there.

I suppose I should be thankful, but I'm not very heroic,

I can't smile with gratitude when my body is on the torture rack.

All I ask, Lord, is that you help me grasp the worth of the hurt twisting inside me, because if I knew that, maybe I'd be able to bear up better, maybe then I wouldn't be so cranky with those I love most.

But no matter what, Lord, just help me to get through today without being too much of a burden.

Max Pauli

Using our sufferings for others

Lord, make us realise that by simply suffering for Jesus' sake and by bearing 'about in our bodies the dying of Jesus' we can often do more for him and for others than we can by being active. It is very hard to understand this, so please make us realise that our very helplessness can be of great use to others if we suffer it with and for Jesus.

Our suffering works mysteriously, first in ourselves by a kind of renewal and also in others who are perhaps far away, without our ever knowing what we are accomplishing . . . Christ on the cross has perhaps done more for humanity than Christ speaking and acting in Galilee or Jerusalem. Suffering creates life. It transforms everything it touches.

Elizabeth Leseur (1866–1914)

In suffering

In the trials of the desert,
In the night of suffering,
In doubt and loneliness,
Men search for you, Lord,
At the same time they curse you!
Have mercy on us.

A French Cistercian nun

Soul of Christ, sanctify me,
Body of Christ, save me,
Blood of Christ, refresh me.
Water from the side of Christ, wash me.
Passion of Christ, strengthen me.
O good Jesus, hear me,
Within your wounds hide me,
Suffer me not to be separated from you.
From the malicious enemy defend me,
In the hour of my death call me and bid me come to
    you,
That with your saints I may praise you for ever and
    ever.
Amen.

Early fourteenth century

Fear in illness

Lord, take away my fear. Perfect love, I know, casts
out fear. Perfect my love so that I know no fear. Amen.

Why me?

Lord, why have I to endure this pain? I just can't understand it! I've done everything I think you've asked me to do and lived a good honest life, and now this! Why, Lord? Why me? I can't understand it any more than your sevant Job did. I can't understand why you do this sort of thing to the people who try to follow you and keep your commandments. It's not much consolation either to look at what happened to your Son, Jesus. Can't you explain your ways just a little for they seem unfair to me, Lord?

Praying when ill

My strength fails: I feel only weakness, irritation and depression. I am tempted to complain and to despair. What has become of the courage I was so proud of, and which gave me so much self-confidence? As well as my pain I have to bear the shame of my fretful feebleness. Lord, destroy my pride; leave it nothing to feed on. I shall be content if you can teach me by these terrible afflictions that I am nothing, that I can do nothing of myself and that you are all!

François Fénelon (1631–1715)

The worst of pain, O Lord, is that it makes it difficult to pray.

Yet, O Lord, I desire to pray, to have communion with you, to draw strength and healing from you, to link to you those whom I love and those who have need of your love; to thank you for those who look after me and those who wish me well.

O Lord, let me always remember that to talk to you is prayer.

George Appleton

Lord, now I am ill I have plenty of time to pray, but I am too taken up with my pain and fears to do more than say, please help me to endure, don't leave me, and remember me when I become so concerned with myself that I forget you. Help me to put myself in your hands even though all I want to do is to complain and resent the suffering. Never let your Spirit cease to pray in the depth of my being, I beg you. Amen.

Short prayers for when ill

Lord help me!

Support and strengthen me Lord!

Lord, help me to keep going.

My Lord and my God.

Lord Jesus Christ have mercy on me, a sinner.

Lord, I offer all my pain against the terrible pain of the world.

Lord, I offer what I suffer for those who suffer without hope.

If you wish it, Lord, you can save me from suffering
   or you can cure me. I do not understand why
   you don't do something but if this is your will,
   so be it.

You bore the pain of the cross; please help me to bear
   this agony.

God of thy goodness, give me thyself, so that I shall
   not lose my way in this suffering.

Trying to understand

Lord, I love you and I trust you, but I do not
understand why I should suffer like this. Give me light
so that I may see, and a loving heart so that I may
comprehend what is happening to me. Do not leave
me now, but give me strength to bear whatever
happens to me, however bewildered I may be. Amen.

Strengthening

Lord, your servant Paul said: 'When I am weak,
then am I strong'. I feel so weak, pray God I may be
strong.

Lord, I call on you as the almighty. You can do all
things. Give me strength against my temptation to
despair.

The Lord is my light and my salvation; whom then
shall I fear? The Lord is the strength of my life; of
whom then shall I be afraid? . . . Hear my voice, O

Lord, when I cry unto thee, have mercy upon me and hear me. I have eyes only for thee; I long for thy presence. My heart says to thee 'Thy face Lord, do I seek'; O hide not thy face from me . . . I believe I will see the goodness of the Lord in the land of the living. Wait patiently on the Lord; be strong and he shall comfort thy heart; put thou thy trust in the Lord.

Adapted from Psalm 27

The Lord is my shepherd
    I shall not want;
He makes me lie down in green pastures.
He leads me beside still waters;
    he restores my soul.
He leads me in paths of righteousness
    for his name's sake.
Even though I walk through the valley of the shadow
        of death,
    I fear no evil;
For thou art with me;
    thy rod and thy staff,
    they comfort me.
Thou preparest a table before me
    in the presence of my enemies;
Thou anointest my head with oil,
    my cup overflows:
Surely goodness and mercy shall follow me
    all the days of my life;
And I shall dwell in the house of the Lord
    for ever.

Psalm 23 (R.S.V.)

Christ be with me, Christ within me,
Christ behind me, Christ before me,
Christ beside me, Christ to win me,
Christ to comfort and restore me,
Christ beneath me, Christ above me,
Christ in quiet, Christ in danger,
Christ in hearts of all that love me,
Christ in mouth of friend and stranger.

Saint Patrick (372-466)

Before going into hospital

Lord, help me, I am dreading going into hospital. There will be no privacy, but people continually about, bustling and noisy. I will never have any peace and quiet in which to pray to you. For even in the night people call out, nurses rush around and talk loudly. Lord, give me a sense of your presence deep within me, and a sense of peace that will persist under all the fuss and bother, for I need your help if I am to remain unflustered and serene.

Hospital

In this ward, Jesus, there are so many who are suffering, some are even dying, some are very alone in their pain. Help us to bear our own cross of anxiety, sickness and loss of faith, so that we may help those around who do not know or love you. Lord, we believe in you and your love for us. Increase our faith and trust.

Before an operation

Jesus, I am very afraid. I do not know what is going to happen to me. I have absolutely no control over what happens and I dislike not being in control. I am afraid of the loss of consciousness that the anaesthetic will bring. I worry that I will be a burden to others after the operation and that I will not be so active again. Lord, help me to trust you. Arrange my life even though it may mean 'my being carried about where I have no wish to go'. (*John 21*) Let me realise if I die now I will be coming to you whose love casts out fear.

Sleeplessness when ill

Lord, I can't go to sleep and there is nothing I want more. I want to escape from my difficulties and yet I know that with your strength it can become a most precious time, your God-given time to pray for all those who in the hours of the night are lost in darkness. Take this darkness from them so that they may know your light.

F.M.

Complaining when ill

Lord, I am sick, in pain, heavily drugged. I want to accept your will and yet when anyone visits me I am tempted to complain endlessly about what is happening to me. Lord, help me to break through this barrier of self, to be alive to the interests, troubles and, above all, the sufferings of others.

F.M.

Fear of death

Lord, you did not seem to want to die—at least not that way. You did ask your father, they tell us, 'let this chalice pass'—but he didn't and I can see why. But 'this chalice', Lord, my chalice, my sickness which they won't tell me is my dying, but which I half know and half dread—if only, if only. There is so much I still want to do, Lord, and I'm afraid. So help me be calm and help me say 'but not my will but thine be done'. Amen.

I love you Lord, and I always thought I longed to see you face to face, but now I am dying I want to cling to life. Help me to overcome the fear of relinquishing this life, and to remember that when I do I will live more fully with you. Be close to me in this difficult time. Amen.

For one whose strength is slow in coming back

O God,
I'm all right so long as I am lying here in bed, or so long as I don't try to do anything; but I have just no strength.
I can't hurry;
I can't even do anything quickly;
I have always to take my time—and it is a long time.
It is so discouraging always to feel weak, and always to feel tired.
I want to get back to work, there is so much that I want to do, and so much that is waiting to be done.

O God,
Give me the patience that I know I must have.
Make me a little better every day until, bit by bit, I
can shoulder the tasks of life again.
The prophet said:
They who wait for the Lord shall renew their strength.

William Barclay

Convalescence

Lord, for weeks and months I have been helpless,
being washed and fed, amused and spoiled, now you
are beginning to give me back your gift of health.
Give me courage to use your strength to take each step
as I am asked, patience to be as slow as you want me
to be, daring to go faster than I feel I can go, and
above all help me to forget myself, the fussed-over
and petted invalid, so that I may become again totally
given to you through others.

F.M.

Prayer of a blind, helpless woman

Lord! I thank thee that in thy love thou hast taken
from me all earthly riches, and that thou now clothest
me and feedest me through the kindness of others.
Lord! I thank thee, that since thou hast taken from
me the sight of my eyes, thou servest me now with the
eyes of others.

Lord! I thank thee that since thou hast taken away
the power of my hands and my heart, thou servest me
by the hands and hearts of others. Lord, I pray for

them. Reward them for it in thy heavenly love, that they may faithfully serve and please thee till they reach a happy end.

Saint Mechthild of Magdebourg (1212–1280)

Going blind

O God,
It is hard to think of a world
    in which I cannot see the sun and the flowers,
    and the faces of those I love.
It is hard to think of a life
    in which I cannot read or watch things,
      or see lovely things any more.
But even in the dark there will be something left.
I can still have memory,
    and I can still see things again
    with my mind's eye.
I thank you for Braille, which keeps the world of books
    from being altogether closed to me.
I thank you that I will still be able to hear the voices I
    know and to touch the things and people I love.
Lord Jesus you are the Light of Life;
    Be with me in the dark.

William Barclay

After a stroke

You've taken away almost everything that I enjoyed, Lord, and most of me. Please use my uselessness.

Deafness

I used to hear so well and loved what I heard, human voices, music, birds, the sound of trains. Now I'm in a silent world, Lord. People shout at me and grow cross when I don't hear. It embarrasses and hurts me and I cannot now enjoy music or nature or anything with my hearing. I pray I may accept it more and learn to use it.

For cheerfulness in illness

Grant, we beseech thee, almighty God, that we, who in our tribulation are yet of good cheer because of thy loving kindness, may find thee mighty to save from all dangers, through Jesus Christ. Amen.

Roman Breviary

Mental suffering

When my heart is as cold as stone and I have neither love to give others nor mercy for my own worthlessness, let me know, at least sometimes, that your love for me is changeless and that I must not despise what you both love and value. Give something of your own invincible courage, and never let me quench my own flickerings of hope.

J.B.P.

I have no longer any control of my thoughts or somehow even of myself. I am overwhelmed by gloom and am in a well of despair, and I cannot lift myself out of it. I suppose I don't even want to, yet I am miserable beyond belief and remaining in it is unending hell. How can you leave me like this, Lord? I cry to you out of the depth of my despair. Give me some glimpse of hope; lift me up out of the depths; send help that will penetrate my gloom, for, Lord, I cannot help myself.

Calm my troubled heart; give me peace.
O Lord, calm the waves of this heart; calm its tempests!
Calm thyself, O my soul, so that the divine can act in thee!
Calm thyself, O my soul, so that God is able to repose in thee, so that his peace may cover thee!

Sören Kierkegaard (1813–1855)

I am lost. There is nothing but darkness on every side. I am close to despair. Jesu, good Shepherd, take my hand. Please. Please. Please.

On the cross, Lord, they gave you vinegar and gall to kill the pain. Lord, please find a way to kill this ache in my whole being.

Lord, when this depression comes on me I am weighed down, all joy leaves me, and I am in a state of melancholy gloom that seems unending. There is no way out. No human care or love touches me. I am shut in. Lord, do not let it come upon me again. If it does, let me know that you are with me in it. Make me realise that you shared this sort of depression on the cross and understand the awfulness from

which one cannot escape. I am held in it as in a vice.
Lord, be with me, let me know that you love me.

Lord, I am very tense and the slightest thing going
wrong makes me want to explode and let fly at people.
Lord, you can heal this hurt in me which makes me so
taut and brittle and which makes me blame other
people for everything. Say to me: 'peace be still' and
help me to let this peace enter into the whole of my
being and thaw out my tenseness.

I said:
'Lord, I cannot bear it,
This constant pain—this constant suffering.
Help me—save me—deliver me;
O heal these wounds!'
He said: 'Be still—be calm—listen for my voice'.
I fell into silence,
And in dark waters I waited for him to speak,
    to say: 'I will heal these wounds,
I will take them from thee'.
I waited—time stood still.
Then, all at once he spoke;
And oh—he said:
'My heart is wounded too'.

Anonymous (modern)

To the Holy Spirit

What is soiled, make thou pure;
What is wounded work its cure;
    What is parched, fructify;

25

What is rigid, gently bend;
What is frozen, warmly tend;
   Strengthen what goes erringly.

Anonymous (13th century)

Thanksgiving for recovery from illness

O God, great, mighty and revered,
In the abundance of thy loving kindness,
   I come before thee
To render thanks
   For all the benefits thou hast bestowed upon me.
In my distress I called upon thee
   And thou didst answer me;
From my bed of pain I cried unto thee
   And thou didst hear the voice of my supplication.
Thou hast chastened me sore, O Lord,
   But thou didst not give me over unto death.
In thy love and pity
   Thou broughtest up my soul from the grave.
For thine anger is but for a moment;
   Thy favour is for a lifetime;
Weeping may tarry for the night,
   But joy cometh in the morning.
The living,
He shall praise thee,
   As I do this day,
And my soul that thou didst redeem
   Shall tell thy wonders unto the children of men.
Blessed art thou,
   The faithful physician unto all flesh.

Authorised Daily Jewish Prayer Book

O tender Father, you gave me more, much more even than I thought to ask. It comes to me that our human desires can never really match what you long to give . . . Thanks, and thanks again, O Father, for having granted me what I asked, and that which I neither knew of nor asked.

Saint Catherine of Siena (c. 1347–1386)

Healing

Lord, there was an occasion in the Gospel when someone called out: 'If it is really your will, make me whole'. And you replied: 'Of course it is! Be whole!' I'm crying out now, Lord. I say if it is your will. Can I take it that it really is? Can I hope and trust? I really mean it, Jesus. Do you?

I lie here day in and day out and watch the world go by. And I feel like the cripple at the pool. Somehow I am never the one selected for healing. But I believe you are the true healer, Lord—sometimes through men and women doctors and others, but sometimes directly. I do not mind how it comes, but Jesus, Son of David, have pity on me. Heal me.

God, the source of all health: so fill our hearts with faith in thy love, that with calm expectancy we may make room for thy power to possess us, and gracefully accept thy healing; through Jesus Christ our Lord.

John W. Suter

Praying with the sick

Be still and comforted; the Lord is with you,
strengthening and supporting you.

Put your trust in him for he loves and cares for you.
Listen to Jesus when he says 'Peace be still' and believe
that he is with you, and will help you always. Amen.

Son of God, in your life you went about healing the
sick and raising the dead. You seemed so much against
suffering, so humanly concerned to remove the burden
of it. In all humility, Lord, we cannot grasp why we
have to go through this. Why us, Lord? We beg you—
stretch out your healing hand and remove this
horror of injury/disease/the threat of death. We really
want this, Lord. We really beg you for healing. You
can do it, Lord. Will you, please? . . . But if not,
Lord, painfully but truly, we will try to say:
'Thy will be done.'

Lord Jesus, heal your servant quickly, if this be
your will. You said to your disciples that you were
leaving peace with them; give N that peace which you
promised; the peace that this world cannot give. Let
not her heart be troubled or afraid. Help her to trust
and to know that you are with her even to the end of
time. Increase the faith of all who follow you, and
help us to love you and each other more deeply. Amen.

Lord, I'm not sick myself, but as I sit beside by this sick friend I want to pray for and with her/him. I don't know what to say. I just want to put this suffering before you Lord, and say: 'Have mercy.'

Lord, as we are here together, one lying on a bed of sickness, the other sitting on the bedside chair, we are each full of pain and distress. Send your healing Spirit to lighten our anxiety, to relieve our suffering, to give us strength to battle on in fighting this disease, in keeping hope and joy alive in our hearts. Lord you loved the sick in your life-time; show us your love now. Amen.

Who shall separate us from the love of Christ? Shall tribulation or distress, or persecutions, or famine, or nakedness, or peril, or sword?

No, in all these things we are more than conquerors through him who loved us. I am convinced that neither death, nor life, nor angels, nor principalities, nor things present, nor things to come, nor powers, nor height, nor depth, nor anything else in all creation will be able to separate us from the love of God in Christ Jesus our Lord. Amen.

Romans 8 (R.S.V.)

Most Holy Trinity, have mercy upon us.
O Lord, cleanse us from our sins.
O Master, pardon our iniquities.
O Holy One, visit and heal our infirmities for thy
 Name's sake.
Lord, have mercy (three times).
Glory be to the Father, and to the Son, and to the
Holy Spirit, both now and ever, into ages of ages.
Amen.

Eastern Orthodox

ACKNOWLEDGEMENTS

The authors and the publishers wish to express their gratitude to the following for permission to include copyright material in this book:

William Collins Sons & Co. Ltd. for prayers from *Prayers for Help and Healing* by William Barclay.

Lutterworth Press for prayers from *Prayers Old and New* by Henry S. Nash.

The Longman Group for prayers from *A Cambridge Bede Book* by Eric Milner-White.

The Society for Promoting Christian Knowledge for prayers from *Jerusalem Prayers* by George Appleton.

Ligouri Publications for prayers from *Prayers for the Time Being* by Max Pauli.

Every effort has been made to trace the owners of copyright material, and we hope that no copyright has been infringed. Pardon is sought and apology made if the contrary be the case, and a correction will be made in any reprint of this book.